Praise for *Path of Totality*

"These poems are blisteringly clear, devastated, and oracular, and they brim with the kindness that comes after terrible enlightenment."　　　　　—SARAH MANGUSO, author of
300 Arguments and *Very Cold People*

"It seems impossible this book was written, and with such grace and startling beauty. Amidst utter devastation and pain—hope, even humor, emerges, and tenderness for others, and for the other-than-human. These poems are the sunflowers growing up through the abyss."

—KATE ZAMBRENO, author of *Drifts*

"This poet speaks from the most terrible grief, losing a child, in the most direct way possible. When language begins to fail, she does not fall silent, but moves into a startling metaphorical knowledge: 'What are you supposed to call the feeling / When you see a star and realize that it corresponds to a map / That it's just one point in a huge map / Extending over everything like an enormous dark skull.' The poems are not often dark or sad. Yet they all feel achieved by means of an utterly terrible price. When I read their harrowing truths, I remember the irrefutable necessity of poetry."　　　　　—MATTHEW ZAPRUDER, author of
Father's Day and *Why Poetry*

"You hold this book but this book also holds you . . . This book is alive, as painful as that might be to its brilliant writer. It's not much comfort but not much can comfort— comfort is not in this universe. What suffuses this universe is all the universe holds despite what, and who, is lost. Am I speaking in code? Any reader of this book knows what I'm saying about it—to the reader nothing, not even utter emptiness, is alien. And emptiness is never utter, though it can be uttered and that sound resembles a splash of stars, a milky wash of stark existence, consciousness, connectedness almost unbearably relentless, almost unbearably beautiful." —BRENDA SHAUGHNESSY, author of *The Octopus Museum*

"The exquisitely lyric *Path of Totality* is as gentle and tender as it is fierce and potent. At the same time, this is not a book about fortitude, hope or overcoming. After the death of a loved one, particularly a child, going through the everyday motions of our remaining lives holds no respite. Every object, place, experience and encounter attaches itself to that loss through remembrances large and small as we fight to integrate the impossible. What we endure in loss is an infinite pain, felt at varying levels of intensity. Echoes of the unimaginable reverberate, both hollow and overwhelming, capturing grief's relentless waves as they crash and break over, over and around us, through this work: 'You can just end up with nothing in return.' Genre feels less important than the shape and shaping of language itself, and *Path of Totality* is a container woven to fit the content perfectly. Grief is messy, and the work does not deny that. But there is nothing chaotic about these poems. They grasp the raw and honorable honesty that deep sorrow demands, and deliver with startling clarity and attention the impossible, unending experience of loss, yes—but also the vast emotional landscape of human experience."

—KHADIJAH QUEEN, author of *Anodyne*

Praise for *Dead Horse*

One of *Flavorwire*'s 50 Best Independent
Press Books of the Year
One of *Paper*'s Must-Read Books of the Year
One of *Entropy*'s Best Poetry Books of the Year

"Her work is startling in its starkness and crisp, distinct voice . . . Pollari's poetry blazes and stings with the intensity and ferociousness of a fresh wound."   —*Publishers Weekly*

"Niina Pollari's poems unfold with a phrasal clarity I didn't know I needed, and which disturbs me: 'like an animal / enjoying the warm sunshine with blood in my mouth.' Her poems deploy the vatic informality of Tytti Heikkinen or Hiromi Ito, indubitably of the present yet of a material insoluble to the present, a voice that issues from a Grecian urn or can of Coors. This is resolved, odd, clear-complicated stuff, lovely 'like a fakey arcade.'"   —JOYELLE MCSWEENEY,
author of *Toxicon & Arachne*

"Niina Pollari's book of poems may appear swift and digestible on the page, but her sparse words are full of weight. These poems—about death, love, sex, blood, and everything else furrowed in your subconsciousness—will send chills down the spine, hit you in the gut, and throw your brain for a loop."   —JINNIE LEE, *Refinery29*

"Pollari's poems, while they may deal with emotional deadness/static/resignation, are extremely corporeal, vibrant, and belong right alongside those of the more well-known 'gurlesque' writers . . . The best way for me to assess this work is to say it oozes a sort of macabre, and yet is incredibly tender and moving. Each poem is like a tiny altar constructed to honor the best kind of sad, the feeliest kind of feels . . . Go! Go love this book to the ground!"
                    —CARLEEN TIBBETTS, *Queen Mob's Teahouse*

Praise for *Total Mood Killer*

"Pardon the punk rock analogy, but: you know how, every once in a while, two great bands will release a split LP where each half is fantastic but the connections between sides turn the whole thing into something greater? This inventive, technology-obsessed work is the poetry version of that, and it's terrific."   —*Vol. 1 Brooklyn*, One of Our Favorite Poetry Books of the Year

Path of Totality

PATH OF TOTALITY

Poems

Niina Pollari

Soft Skull
New York

Library of Congress Cataloging-in-Publication Data
Names: Pollari, Niina, author.
Title: Path of totality : poems / Niina Pollari.
Description: First Soft Skull edition. | New York : Soft Skull, 2022.
Identifiers: LCCN 2021021740 |
ISBN 9781593767037 (paperback) | ISBN 9781593767044 (ebook)
Subjects: LCGFT: Poetry.
Classification: LCC PS3616.O56836 P38 2022 | DDC 811/.6—dc23
LC record available at https://lccn.loc.gov/2021021740

Cover design by www.houseofthought.io
Book design by tracy danes

Published by Soft Skull Press
New York, NY
www.softskull.com

Printed in the United States of America
1 3 5 7 9 10 8 6 4 2

For Lumi. I love you so much.

Contents

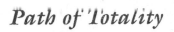

Path of Totality

People Have Sad Stories

People have sad stories. The husband died, the baby died. Or they didn't die; they just stayed sick. For a long long time. Eventually they died. The pearl scraped off, the ring sunk deep into edema.

In the photo, my face smiles. The lighting is executive, flattering. But the granules of my skin have no sweetness. They have spent their money. I touch my face when I go to sleep and it is like someone is touching me. Eventually I tip backward. Then it's another one.

You can just end up with nothing in return. Four quarters get you a tall can of iced tea at the gas station, and then you walk off into the night. Time gets into a car like a glamorous woman in a raincoat. Lapel so big you don't see the woman. But she's there. Or she was, for a little while.

The funeral director came to your apartment, a big question mark over her head. She had a plastic box. You wanted her to like you. Why?

Today it rained all afternoon. I ate the lunch I brought instead of the one I wanted.

My husband is alive. The fist of my heart almost unclenched itself, but I caught it.

If I say a word twice, that doesn't mean it's negative. I love you. No, I love love you.

How to Read This Poem

In this poem we don't remember the past

The past is like dark water

Around an algae bloom

It holds the whole thing together

Parts of the bloom cling together

Appearing as one organism

But spreading individually

Like the heavy influence

Of a cohesive group

The water around it

Always invisibly moving

Looks like the same water

But it's new water

Or maybe a mixture of old and new

This way permutations of the past

Can approach us again

And we don't notice

I have a hard time saying *we* in poems

Since I don't think I can tell you anything

But I can say this

We are not smart

Maybe what I mean is

I am not smart and I want you to know

That if you feel you also aren't

Then I understand

Today I forgot the spaghetti at the grocery store

Even though I went specifically for it

Now I feel totally defeated

And I want to put my face on the ground

I eat my entire hoard of resources

Absently and without decision

I don't want to think about my own death

I just want to get metaphysically larger

Accumulate more trinkets

Blot out everything else

Though never on purpose

I pull a long hair out of a jewelry box

The last time I opened the box was years ago

The hair is a relic of a person

With assumptions about her own freedom

A person who always took the last chair

And pretended to lose herself in the reading

Or whatever she was attending

Someone calculating

Married to the exit

I'm not saying

That I've totally changed

That lived experience makes you more real

Or that you need to be sad in order to make things

But I recall myself from years ago like an image

Of someone I no longer wish to be around

I wind the found hair around my finger

Until the circulation slows just a little

And then I unwind it again

My finger is years older

But the hair is the age from before

And both are somehow mine

In this poem nobody is a killer

Even though we have all killed before

Ruthlessly or absentmindedly or out of fear

The spider you smashed with a book

That threw its front legs up

Before you flattened it

Its protest so human

That you thought about it for days

Remembering yourself as newly ruthless

And despite the spider

This poem contains no killers

But neither is anyone in this poem

Known as a victim

Though we have all held our shoes in the cooling night

And waited for a taxi and maybe cried

And when the cabbie stops for cigarettes

At the gas station and asks you if you need anything

You say no but it feels like a lie

This poem is enormous in scale

And every element is here in it

Its ambition is staggering

It contains a hurricane

An earthquake

A huge fucking flame

That would destroy everything you love

Emotionlessly and efficiently

The rain that comes down

The clean hospital window

Until you feel like you're in a flood

And the flood is like the water

Draining over the earth's edge

And you float across the map

Like you might fall off it

Everything powerful

Enough to destroy you

Is right here in this poem

And you are so puny

After you get wounded

Your little fingertips

Touch your little wound

Like the incredulous Saint Thomas

Thrown apart by the idea

That anything bad could happen to you

And this poem is here to remind you

Of all the things you can't control

How they seem like magic

Or bad magic

But aren't

Sometimes what you need is to imagine

Your memories taking a different shape

Or changing and becoming different memories

In order to let them sink into your skin

Like an emollient

At first it's superficial

And of dubious benefit

But you do it because you believe

In its power to make you better

And over the weeks

As you look in the mirror

You can convince yourself

That it has

In this poem you can think

Of the memories you never had

Till they feel like memories you really had

And in this poem

It's fine

To have had those memories

Life Force

Let people see you from a distance.

Outside they stand on a dune, looking down. Inside they stand on a ladder, going up somewhere, and then they look back at their sad friend sitting in the middle of the living room.

In the restaurant, you fork a salad around a plate, move the pieces into your mouth. They feel like pieces of a dollar bill, going down your throat like you're being paid. When you eat something, you take it apart with your body. You reject most of it, but some of it has to be made into you. This is like grief.

My friend goes, "Hey, I'm sorry I haven't been in touch . . ."

My husband read a book about how money is a life force, and you get to choose when to give it away. The bills I receive ask for even more money. I pay for iron pills, I pay for stool softener. But there is a bill I received that I still have not paid. Months pass.

Seven months have passed at the time of this dispatch.

I choose not to give away any more of my life force.

I am the one with the power.

Halloween

I once wrote a poem about learning to trust. It was a complete fiction; I don't trust anyone. But now I attend a support group. We pass around cards or flowers. I see everyone's face and I look at their relic.

A cut flower is a dead flower. A star can be dead or alive; you don't know from afar. You can buy someone a star and name it after them and you don't know if it's alive or dead. But behind everyone who walks into a room is a centipede of their pasts. If they walk onto a train and ride, so do their pasts.

We could have met each other so long ago, and almost did. But in this life we had to meet in this room, over this pitcher of water, our faces dredged like this.

I am dropped into two timelines.

What kind of music will you want to play, the funeral director asks. That kind of music doesn't exist. She puts on something very quiet, and the light falls into the room like a dotted line.

When I was small, I had rabbits. They were eaten. When I was small, I had kittens. My sister strangled one. She didn't mean to, but she held it too tightly and I saw. If I see some-thing, does that mean I am trusted with the information?

There is a dog that lurks in the corners instead of cross-ing the room diagonally. A dog that is not asleep, but pre-tending.

I am not working on it, though I say I am.

I saw dust on the piano. Was there a piano? Dust landed so hard it made holes.

It's midday, Halloween. Thirteen days ago I saw the small-est hand.

Love

Sometimes your love becomes too big to be contained by your own body, so you decide to have a baby. Your love expands from its container into this new, second container; love fills up the baby and you. When everything goes as it's meant to go, the baby emerges and you can nestle together at home, letting the love envelop you. But if your baby dies, your love goes searching for someplace to go. It spreads and spreads, not finding its desired object, until it is a thin film that covers the entire world. This way, eventually, your love comes back to itself.

After she died, for weeks I kept getting electric zaps throughout my body—moments of shock that I couldn't account for, little dumps of adrenaline that jolted me back. I sat on the couch, staring out at the bird feeder my husband zip-tied onto the fire escape; I could lose hours this way. But the jolts would shock me back into the room. I came to think of them as a kind of location device. My body was dumb, and it didn't know what had happened. My dumb body was trying to find the baby. I described these jolts to my sister. That used to happen to me too, she said. She had a live baby; her baby, when small, had been right there at her breast, but her body had still zapped her, as if to remind her to be vigilant in love.

I had a pregnancy book I'd been filling out. I'd shied away from filling in the details until we'd passed the twelve-week mark, the point at which pregnancies become statistically less likely to miscarry. I'd been afraid of filling it in because of the risks, before. But now, afterward, I feel differently. Now I think: Why not throw yourself wholeheartedly into loving? Love every detail. Love every day. You can't control the outcome; we are all careening. If our plans go the way we want them to go, we congratulate ourselves for being good at planning, but in reality we are just very, very lucky.

In the night, overwhelmed, I held my husband or he held me. Sometimes I curled up and he wrapped his body around mine, and sometimes I pressed my front to his broad back. We were the same physical size for many weeks; he was losing weight, and I was still holding on to mine, my postpartum body watery and adjusting. We were containers, and we were waiting for our love to return.

At the Drowned Valley

I need you

But I can't talk right now

I know you understand

Let's go down to the river

Like a pair of convalescents

Let's walk slowly toward the gray river

And when we get there

Let's open our eyes

Which have been closed for days

And we can regard the gray water

As it pulls listlessly down toward the bay

Let the air throw birds around like manuscript pages

Let my pain radiate from me like skin cells sloughing

Like an automatic process

And as I clasp my hand into yours

Let's close the emptiness between our palms

And force out the distance

Till there isn't one

Compassion

People eat animals. I sometimes do. I eat sardines that are packed side by side. I forget about their swimming when I do this.

But they are pulled from the ocean and put into a tin.

Once you asked someone to describe a typical day of eating for them. Now, when you think of this person, a part of you is always thinking of what they routinely eat.

Once you were given a drink that had a whole egg in it. A yolk casually emulsified into alcohol. Then a white slipped in and shaken. And you drank it down as if it was nothing.

You have to eat, the nurse said. We have to see you eat. The staff brought me rolls, vegetable soup, a pudding cup. One of my actions of mothering, for nine months, had been to eat. Afterward, I didn't want to eat because it was only for me.

There's an animal rights protest in Union Square. People wear overalls made of netting over their regular clothes. The overalls hover around their bodies like auras while they circle carcasses on a tarp. The carcasses are the bodies of lambs and chickens and dogs. The people scoop them up like they are beloved.

A Story About the Nature of Time

A long time in the past, a door opens. Four young men carry a gurney with a living body on it out of a building. The body is wrapped in a sheet, and bleeds onto a disposable mat. The body's fingers hold the mat in place. Its face looks toward the sky, where there is no rain, only an empty eye.

The men step down the stairs like large show horses, in unison. The oil they emit from their bodies dissipates into the air in a metallic spritz. They put the body into a vehicle, then take it to an emergency room, where it is scraped. Its liquids are low like a receding tide. Before it goes under, it feels its death drive beat inside it like a live fetus.

The body wakes up, receives a bag of blood, eats iron. The iron travels through the body like a benevolent knight. The body doesn't even have to acknowledge it's being repaired.

Leaning on the power of the iron, the body can rise like a shitty tower. The body climbs a StairMaster at the gym, rising above everyone else.

The body has dreams, even now.

White Blood Cells

I have a new skin. It's a veil of plasma that grows over a wound. White blood cells rise to my surface like pearl divers. Their lungs are bursting.

My new skin is tender and sensitive. When people walk past me, I feel the breeze of their passing. It gives me a shiver like something that's about to happen.

Before you say anything, I can feel your question leaving your body and coming toward me like an odor that you release. It walks up to my door. It kicks over my talisman with its soft feet.

When I decided to have her, I made myself into a home. Now her huge home is like a prolapsed organ. It's bigger than I am. I can inhabit it too. I inflate it until it takes shape, a rising bouncy castle. Then I wander its rooms.

If you wear yourself like clothes, then you are naked all the time.

Put me full of someone else's blood. Let me wander my own rooms, and be my own contents. What I contain is disgusting. What I contain might come out anytime. It might be ruby. It might be dark. It might be a butter yellow. You don't know.

I practice saying "Yes, I have a daughter." But when I open my mouth, something else starts to come out. I suck it back in. I hope nobody will ever ask, but then I hope someone asks. I hope more than anything.

Urine Season

Summer in New York is urine season. Everything has an odor. The hot rain comes and hoses down the sidewalk, but the smell remains, floating there as warmth on live skin. People toss bottles out of their cars, and the bottles explode over the sidewalk. Or they stay closed and roll to a stop, then cook for days next to an architecturally famous building.

Last time it was urine season, I was expecting. That's how you say it. You don't say what you're expecting. I didn't know what I expected, but now I know. I held my pee on every corner of this town, waiting to meet my daughter.

This year I've been watching a livestream of a falcon nest. On a ledge above the sidewalk are three falcon hatchlings. They wait and watch in their rocky nest, knowing that their parents will bring them smaller birds to eat. There were four eggs in the nest, but the fourth didn't hatch. The three remaining hatchlings grow larger and more dangerous each day. They rip apart tanagers and starlings as they learn the ways of predation. They shit over the edge of the building. The excrement drips down the side.

Today the falcons left.

This is a poem about expectation.

At the hospital, I had a catheter. It leaked on the bed, on the sheets, against my legs. Someone came in and asked where my baby was, not seeing the decal on the door. I have never felt as helpless.

It's urine season again. It will be again and again. We will feel this way again.

Some will say this is not a poem for them. But I say it's a poem for anyone who ever expected anything.

Self-Portrait as New York Geography

A polluted estuary

With the prosaic name East River

Creeps against the shoreline

Let me describe the sky to you

The sky is high and creamy-metallic with birds like vanilla
  flecks

On the other side the monoliths stand crowded and vertical

It's beautiful if you have the capacity to appreciate beauty

It's beautiful like order

Or like the satisfaction

Of a met expectation

Long ago the river flooded

And reached its fingers deep into the coast

Any geometry we've given the shore

Comes from human effort

Wall Street is filled in with animal remains

Garbage, sand, and concrete

Then built upon

As if where it stands

Was always there

That's the trick

Build something gleaming enough

Sink enough money into it

And nobody will even remember

That when it started out

It was just trash and offal

Here on the other side

Condo developers have claimed all the best views

And you have to stand very close to the river

To see the water at all

The light is even

I'm behind sunglasses

Even though it's sunless

I'm covering my eyes

Because cosmetically speaking I am in ruins

To look at my face directly would inspire nervousness

The way that looking at an abandoned or burned building

Would make a person want to lock their doors

I feel like the opposite

Of the Financial District

I feel as if my foundation is solid

But everything else has been built from bodies

I feel like a mountain of discarded parts

I draw scavengers

Great funnels of turkey vultures

Like the guy who pointed his camera

When they wheeled me into the ambulance

And filmed me as his German shepherd sniffed the grass

His face a blank stare even as I told him to go fuck himself

I don't know what to do

I want to lock myself into my apartment

But I also want to flood the plain with the untreated
    sewage of my sadness

I don't have enough money to feel sad for as long as I want
    to feel it

I would like to sleep here on this bench and let the
    weather erode me

But I have to arrange my body back onto the subway

And go under the river to the city

And enter its black buildings like vertical grave
    markers

Sorry this metaphor is so on the nose

And if you're still following well thanks

When the Desolation Comes

Happiness is real only once you leave it behind. But why would anybody leave it.

Once I went down the stairs, and when I came back up, I was different.

Where are you, darling? I'm here.

A successful movement in a poem is surprising. But this is not.

It's cruel to expect surprise from me.

I hope when the desolation comes for you and grips you by the wrist and flings you into the night, you happen to be clutching your insurance paperwork.

Last Summer

Last summer was hot

The eighth hottest in New York

But the personally hottest for me

The boiling air was down my throat

The blistering air was down my stomach

It went into my pores and scooped out each sweat drop

And rolled it down my face and down my back

Like it was bowling with cloudy water

I wobbled down the street

Or I sweated on the couch

Fan pointed at my torso

A huge disgusting mammal

Particulates from the air gathered on me

And mixed with sunblock into a greasy film

In the shower the skin between my toes rubbed off in
    dirty pills

And I scrubbed to get the odor of my hair to disappear for
    five minutes

And I scrubbed the bell of my pregnant abdomen to keep
    it from itching

And when I was done scrubbing

I sat in the tub with the cool water running over me

And I watched it run down the drain

And I thought

This part is going to be over soon

And it will have been so worth it

Pain and Suffering

In the birth class, the teacher explained that birth involved pain but not crisis. That pain was not the same thing as suffering. That we're used to thinking of pain and suffering together, but they were not synonymous and did not always go together.

In the room, my husband and I practiced what we'd do when I began to feel pain. He pressed against my body in different ways as I tried to imagine being in pain but holding suffering at arm's length.

That I would not be suffering. That I would be in pain, but I would not suffer.

I felt I knew it, and I was ready.

But the suffering that did come was too big for me to hold.

I could not hold it in my arms, so I balanced it on my soft new belly. I could not hold it, so I gave it to my husband to hold. I could not hold it, so I put it in the car seat. I could not hold it, so I put it in the crib.

At night the suffering spread over the bed and dripped into the floorboards. In the daytime it opened behind me like a wake as I slowly walked to the waterfront. The suffering seemed to come from me, but it was everywhere. This is not an exaggeration.

I have already forgotten the pain.

Hungry Ghost

When we met to sign the paperwork

It was in a coffee shop called Hungry Ghost

The paperwork consisted of two certificates

And when the funeral director handed them to us to sign

Her face was grim with practiced empathy

Hungry Ghost is a term from Buddhism

For beings who are driven by need

And unlike regular ghosts

Hungry ghosts died in unusual circumstances

Or in their lifetime did an evil deed

Why this is a name for a coffee shop

I don't understand

As much as I don't understand

Why we chose to meet the funeral director there

She had offered to bring the certificates to our apartment

But my immediate reaction was to say no

That I didn't want her inside my home

Though I would later allow her in

But not yet

Hungry Ghost was full of people on laptops

Doing the ordinary work of their lives

Scrubbing through film clips

Or editing an endless document

Like this one

All the tables were taken

So we sat in a row of three on a bench

A large painting of a bull behind us on the wall

The funeral director, my husband, and me

I ordered a small caffeine-free tea

I needed to order something

To pretend we were there

For a normal reason

On this day in October

Just days after my daughter

Came out of me not breathing

I sat behind the barrier of my husband

So that I could hide my face if I needed to

And he covered me with his huge emotional wingspan

Even though he was also feeling devastation

And as I signed the paper

I screamed in the silent forest of my heart

And the queen's corpse

Which was my corpse

Rattled with the force of my voice

I gave the paper back

And held my undrunk tea

In my freezing hands and felt its heat

Radiate into the little calcium of my bones

I had been to Hungry Ghost the day before the birth

I had been feeling good

The contractions were occasional

But already strengthening

I sat with my longtime friend

Who used to tell me

When we were kids

That I was too secretive

That I should feel okay about letting people in

When I'm having a hard time

That I should let people care about me

The way that I care about them

She had the barista take a picture of us

While she pointed at my belly

I saw the photo only once

But I remember exactly

The way it looked

The way I looked in it

Dear friend

I am having

A hard time today

Embarrassment

From the moment I woke up from the anesthesia, I felt overwhelmingly sad—a hopeless wall of sadness. A dead end. A polar darkness. Sadness of an almost incomprehensible scale pressed against my body as I recovered my thoughts. Sadness syncopated through my veins, pressed by the pneumatic compression cuffs that thrummed around my legs to keep my blood from clotting. The first words I spoke were to my doula, who was there because my husband was with the baby: *What am I going to do.* When my husband was finally allowed in to see me, the first thing I said to him was *I'm so sad.*

But a second emotion descended, too: embarrassment. It mingled with despair to become another color, like paint blended on a palette into a custom shade. I felt embarrassed to call my family. I felt embarrassed when the nurses walked in and looked at me with their eyes full of clinical sympathy. I felt embarrassed at how I hadn't seen the trajectory by which I would end up in a public hospital in South Brooklyn without my beloved baby. In the weeks after, I walked through my tilted reality, and despair and embarrassment followed me like two loyal dogs, licking the palms of my hands to let me know they were there every time I paused.

Embarrassment was something I could not express when someone asked me how I was feeling. My mouth wouldn't open to say what I meant—I couldn't force the word out. I remember articulating it only once, weeks after, to a counselor who ran office hours for bereaved parents at a hospital uptown. When I said that I felt embarrassed, I thought I saw her startle, though I don't know if I was projecting this response onto her because I thought that my admitting to feeling it was monstrous. She went on to say that what I was feeling was normal, but I didn't believe her after I thought I'd seen the glimmer of astonishment on her face. *What you're feeling is normal* sounded like a line a counselor is supposed to say to the person they're counseling; hearing it didn't make me feel less freakish. When my husband and I left that office, I said it was good that we had gone, but I didn't feel that it was.

Let me explain all the ways in which I felt embarrassed, even though it embarrasses me to say them. I felt embarrassed because I had let myself feel celebration and hope and joy, even though I now felt that I should have known better. I felt embarrassed that I had let everyone else know that a life as a mother to a live baby was something I desired. I felt embarrassed of my own certainty, which now felt foolish. I felt embarrassed that I would have to inform the world that what I desired was not going to be given to me, and that I had been let down. And I felt embarrassed of the embarrassment itself, as it centered my experience, and thus seemed selfish.

I've looked it up many times online, and found bewildered postpartum people writing on forums, asking why they felt embarrassed about losing their babies, asking whether anyone else felt that way. I've found that the tendency of the responders in the comments is usually to say *You have nothing to be embarrassed about.* This is because most of the responders have babies who are alive. Grief is complicated. *What you're feeling is normal.* I don't believe you.

Miranda Popkey writes in her novel *Topics of Conversation*: "To indicate interest is already to expose oneself to humiliation. To admit the existence of a desired object, to admit that the desired object's disappearance . . . even if only in death, will be painful." Pregnancy is a public ritual, made public by the body's betrayal of intent by growing. By participating in it, I had already indicated interest in witnessing myself as a mother; the death of my baby was a humiliation of my desire.

The word *embarrass* has its roots in the Portuguese *baraço*, noose or rope. The false cognate *embarazada*, meaning "pregnant" in Spanish, is also a descendant of this word; some believe it to be tied to a custom of pregnant women wearing a rope or piece of cloth around their midsections. Embarrassment is, etymologically speaking, already tied to the public acknowledgment of pregnancy.

So why did I feel so alone?

There Is No Word

I wanted to write a true poem.

I started with a fact: She had soft hair. I know because I touched my chin to it when I held her.

The truth is that when I held her, neither of us cried.

A fetus passes its genetic material to its mother beginning at six weeks' gestation. The mother carries it with her even when the fetus, now a child, parts from her body. The mother becomes a genetic chimera, feeling as if her children are with her even when they are not.

When I was a small child, I walked with my day-care provider across a street every day to a playground. Down the street there was a church whose roof was being leafed with bright copper. Later, the copper roof oxidized to a matte green. It surprised me because I didn't understand yet that some changes are chemical, irreversible.

The truth is that inside a car, driving past a field where dusk almost touches the ground, sometimes you can see a shooting star as it burns green and falls. The copper of its body lights on fire as it enters this atmosphere. It is visible only for a short time, and then it's gone.

I walk through the body of every day like an organism be-
ing born. Through the red gel and muck of the underbelly.
Through all the female pain.

I say I walk but in truth there is no word for the locomotion
that I do.

Facts and Memories

All I have are facts and memories. Facts are things that cannot be changed, and memories are impressions of a time when I did not yet know my own face contorted like this.

Facts are: Her weight and length.

Memories are: My loneliness.

After the fact, I invent a narrative. I see the story, its rising action, its fall. We all do this.

The light at dawn was a gradient rising from beyond the dark apartment buildings like the cape of a Vegas performer. She inhaled before she turned to face her audience. I was alone, but have a picture I took on my phone. Is this a fact or a memory?

When I was laboring, I took four or five showers. In the shower, each time I had a contraction, I yelled "Now," and my husband started the timer. The log of the timer still exists, the final contraction appearing to go on for hours, my husband never having pressed stop, proof of time spinning out of our hands.

Maybe it did go on for hours. Maybe it's still going on.

I remember the hot water and how it abated my pain. Does revisiting the memory now, knowing what I know, change the way in which the water helped me?

My husband put frozen blueberries into my mouth, one by one, when I couldn't think anymore. I felt their coldness in my mouth as I sank backward into my body.

My husband put my socks and shoes on my feet, and slowly we walked down the stairs.

I'm Sorry

I want to apologize. I'm sorry that I have had to pull you down with me into this antechamber full of cold blood bags. It's hard to believe such a room exists, that there is really a room where they just put bags of blood. But they stack up and stack up. When I got here, they didn't cover the door, but they do now. I don't think anyone ever comes for the blood bags again. No, really. It's drafty. I'm so sorry.

Hold one of the bags, and feel the blood inside.

This is my mothering instinct talking.

I'm sorry for how this ends, in a chamber that used to lead somewhere.

Obligatory Hematophage

I walk through the grass. A tick lands on me, and I feel its feeding structure penetrate me like an expression of empathy. I could keep going like this. I could keep being taken from.

The tick's anticoagulant makes me high. I see colors I couldn't see before. I sense the odors of the world, and they are reddish and brown.

I remember my last blood meal. It was much more than I thought I could eat, but I ate it compulsively, with the fondness of a carnivore. Somewhere in my genetic material, I knew I needed the blood meal in order to change, to move to the next stage of my being. Thanks to the blood meal, I am now further along than I ever was.

The grass is always greener on the other side. The grass is longer. Deer walk through it. Humans walk through it too. I cast my watery eye toward the grass and feel desire with my whole flat body.

Now I can feel that it's my season at last. I land and I attach. I pick where the skin is thinnest. I do it fast.

Ursa Minor

Loneliness is an unlimited resource. Dip into it. Keep dipping.

In another universe I am happy. In this one, I shut my eyes against the oncoming day and feel my happiness peeled from me. My eyes cover over with a film. I start to think a single thought, but before I can finish, it catches flame like silvergrass on the gray hillside. Underneath the flame, hundreds of millipedes curl and desiccate. They turn fetal. They boil away.

Cloud obscures the mountain. Lightning blanches the whole of its interior. White bones, white blood.

And Ursa Minor above the thunderheads, dipping into the cold universe. Up there it's so thin. Even feelings can't stay together. Their atoms drift from one another until they are too far for their gravity to hold.

My love, how can I tell anybody what I mean? That you were born, and that I held you. That when you were born, I was the one who died. That when I died, you were the one who went under and pulled me up again and dressed my body.

How can I tell anybody what I mean?

That I didn't know I would have to love you like this.

That I didn't know we had to die to meet.

Interim

In the interim before the disaster, I transform into the god-head. The transformation is so easy it's almost aesthetic: Suddenly I exude an amniotic appeal and leave trails of cervical mucus that allow me to be followed. My nipples are targets. My body's hairs are individual like lovingly made line drawings. I am full of blood and food.

Being the godhead gives me a voice that is many whispers driven into one voice. It makes me compelling to everyone I address. It's just like listening to the woman of your dreams.

And you know what the disaster is—you have seen it in your own dreams. A mountaintop blows inward like a face hit with a fire extinguisher. The brown cantaloupes roll into the acid ocean.

But the good news is that I can save us all so easily.

This poem is not insane.

In the interim before the disaster, we can hear the thunder and look upon the signage as it illuminates letter by brass letter:

Live Laugh Love

And we can recognize ourselves for what we really are.

Path of Totality

Something set you into motion. A chain of events. Rain falling into a series of cups on a chain, then into a small yard where a small ecosystem drinks it.

Something set you into motion. The love I felt for your father when we drove past the mountain house and snapped a few blurred pictures. We talked about the house the whole drive back to New York. The house, a few weeks later, belonged to us. Its dusty corners, its mice in the refrigerator motor.

Something set you into motion. When we signed the documents, we were in the path of totality. To you, to ourselves after we had known you.

From the day of the eclipse, I began, though you wouldn't form in me for months. But I pledged you my fat and the eyebrows from my face.

On the day of the eclipse, we watched the sky until a hole formed in it and absorbed us. We watched the sky until there was a navel in the universe, and I traveled through it like a nutrient into your veins. Small vessels formed between us. A web formed, drops gleaming on it from my intent. Your fingers, still ghostly, broke the surface tension when they reached from the ether to touch it.

Sorrow

Sorrow is etymologically linked to *sorry* and *sore*.

When I'm sad, I'm sorry.

The sorriness swells.

It comes in under the windows of the hotel where I'm
    staying to get away.

It wets my linens and soaks my packed suitcase.

I have to leave my room in a state of undress.

I am so sorry that I climb onto the roof of the hotel and
    wait for someone to rescue me.

On another day the sorriness tries a different entry.

It seeps up like oil in the basement of my thoughts.

If I open the door the smell hits me, unearthly, inorganic.

I shut the door again but I can't stop thinking about it.

Sometimes I am so sorry that I am sore.

I am so sore that the soreness causes a cancer.

Malignant cells across the larynx so I can no longer speak.

Heart cancer, sarcomas.

I'm always told it's extremely rare, the doctor has never
    seen anything like this before, this affects one in
    200,000 people at the very most.

I take zero comfort in the statistics.

I fall into the dreamless sleep of palliative medical care.

Then I die of the cancer, and then I'm really sorry.

Then the sorrow puts on scrubs.

It reaches into me, a gloved hand, and twists.

It pulls out an organ in pieces, and says something I can't
    hear.

The Frog

In school, I dissected a frog. It lay on its back in front of me, smelling like formaldehyde, on the black table of the lab. In my hand I held the sharpest instrument I was allowed to have. With it I cut, and then I peeled back the skin and looked inside.

My lab partner, a fidgety rich boy, wanted to know if I was a virgin. He looked at me and adjusted his scrotum, waiting for an answer. Before us the frog lay opened. Someone with nothing at stake will always ask you for your intimate details.

But I was a student careless with a body, and when I finished looking, I discarded the body in the waste. I walked from the classroom and I kept walking. I walked through my whole life as if I was somehow more valuable. I gave my body away for nothing to people who do not remember me.

At home, I cut my skin, the skin of my ankle, the skin of my leg. I looked at a website where people posted pictures of their own cuts. The skin cut to the dermis, the fat underneath like a layer of sauce. I carved a symbol onto my ankle to remind myself of something. I've forgotten what I was supposed to recall.

When I was sixteen, a gynecologist looked inside me, and when he was done, he slipped his finger inside my anus. He did this without explaining what he was going to do or why. It might have been a part of the exam. I didn't ask; I simply put my clothes on and drove away. This isn't big, but does it have to be?

Someone with nothing at stake will want every piece of information from you, and they will want it for free.

When I became pregnant, I was reminded every day of the being that I was. I knew the sex of my baby, but when people asked, I pretended I didn't know. As I purchased a greeting card, a man at the counter told me I was having a boy. I smiled and said "Well, let's see," even though I knew he was wrong.

In the bright classroom, the frog's body had been intimate and geometric. Its armpits, its crotch. I can't believe I didn't recognize it.

If a poem is a looking inside of something, I've been dissecting all my life. And for what?

I left behind so many bodies, even my own. I walked away from myself, and the body I used to own was taken somewhere. Someone else said "Open," and then they cut.

I Am Not in the Mood for Strangers

White surfaces

Reflect more heat than darker surfaces

Which absorb the heat instead

This is called the albedo effect

The Arctic and Antarctic regions

Are the largest white spots of the earth

They send heat back into space simply by existing

The melt of these ice sheets will cause more heat to collect

To be absorbed by the ocean and the land, which are
    darker masses

And therefore more receptive to heat

Today it is hot in New York and I am unhappy

My unhappiness comes from my small human reasons

But I am not a heat-resistant animal

So you could say that Arctic ice melt

Also contributes directly to my mood

I want to find a better way to be connected

To this vulnerable planet

Where I struggle

Or find a spasm of happiness

I leave bread out for the birds

I watch as a beige-cheeked house finch

Tears apart a piece of Trader Joe's multigrain loaf

And I feel like I've touched the world today

Even though what I've done is so small

In the Lars von Trier movie *Melancholia*

Which is about a planet that will imminently strike ours

And presumably wipe out human existence

And is also a metaphor for depression

One of the main characters, Justine, says

"The earth is evil, we don't need to grieve for it

Nobody will miss it"

And she's right

Nobody will

Our selves are little icebergs

Bereft on the ocean

And when they have calved

And when they have melted

There will be no selves

In the way we think about selves

Just small hardy animals adapted to thrive in bad shit

Who will rifle through our remaining things and
    repurpose them

Who will tear through our remaining bones and
    repurpose them

And they will not miss the earth

That we were simultaneously so precious

And so cavalier about

The Devil Is Standing Between Me and the Life I Want

I don't believe in the devil but there the devil stands. In the doorway to the bathroom, in the doorway to the bedroom. The devil dwells in doorways because exits are the devil's domain. One more step and the devil is in the bedroom. The devil could fall on the bed, and swell there like an organ.

The devil is here.

I feel it in my organs, and bloom with embarrassment.

The bouquet inside of me is already wilting. I know how this sounds. The devil buries his nose in it, and the action makes me weep because I'm not used to gestures of tenderness.

Every day brings a new tyranny.

I'm on my knees, just like the devil said.

When was the last time I was completely able to look myself in the eye? I could tell you the color, back then. I could skim my hand across my own body and not linger. I could leave a room without making eye contact.

Those days the summer was the point, and the fall was its ending. Now I don't look forward to anything. I just supplicate until I'm completely flat. Flat enough to slide under the door. And it doesn't even feel like an exit.

The devil holds the thing I want. In the doorway. I tell myself there's no malice in his gaze, but I know what kind of exchange this is.

I'm the One Who Loves You

And when I attempt to say who I am

To grant myself permission

Out comes dust

I am trying to say

Out come the remnants

And as of the day you left me

Have all my attempts been negated

Have all my messages been intercepted

Yet left unresponded

Interfered with and destroyed

Delicate paper notes burning

Like master recordings in a warehouse fire

Only copies that curl and shrink

Until there is absolutely nothing left

But dust and again

We emerge from the warehouse

To the same restless world

And then the quiet breaks

Outside in the tree

There's a large crow

It bows like a dinosaur

From the force of its own craw

And I wonder if the gesture

As addendum to the noise

Is voluntary or not

My own hands clench

And then open again

As I turn again and again

And see me in the mirror

Skin the pale blue of a new mushroom

A glow in my eyes like a cursed gemstone

And I remember what happened

And I can't stop turning like this

I'm stuck rotating toward the realization

Like a houseplant mechanically seeking sun

The Spanish word for sunflower

Translates to "turning toward the sun"

I pivot my own leaves

And something keeps turning me away

The cool morning

The afternoon the night

Especially the night

I sweat awake in the sheets

The glands in my armpits aflame

Reaching their fingers into my breast tissue

The night is rattled around me

It's full of alive things

You're not alive

You never visit me in my dreams

Only these hallucinatory animals visit me

Spiders that swing down at me in greasy knots

And hover over me and then swing to the walls

And skitter away disjointed

Nightmare shapes

I try to get smaller to escape them

But my heart gives me away

Its pace

Its constancy

Am I asleep

Is this animal feeling real

This feral oppression

Today my watch stopped recording my heart rate

I was so used to checking it that I thought something was
  wrong with my heart

It was more plausible than the piece of technology
  malfunctioning

The breakable heart in me

Doing its stupid motion

A nodding bird

A bobblehead

Of course it's going to stop

Of course hearts stop

Yours did

Sweetheart

I'm the archetype

Searching in the twilight

Sweeping clay on the banks with my ragged hair

Looking for the bones that I know were pulverized

That I know were sent away in a fire

I looked up and saw the invisible smoke

In the stacks above the crematorium

On that beautiful sunny day

Later the funeral director

Came inside the apartment with them

As I tried not to cry

I know where they are

But I still look for them

So I can arrange them

Into the shape I will always know

The forlorn truth about me is

That I'm the one who loves you

I have no belief

I have no rage

I just do this

I just have to

No Redemption Arc

No more stories can be good. No more stories have a redemption arc.

The forest where we used to picnic is ash.

Last winter someone murdered a bear in its den and it was perfectly legal.

I sit near a small fire telling my selfish tale to everyone who gathers. I clutch myself and yell like I'm from an ancient culture that values mourning. But I'm a curiosity, and the badness of my story is unexceptional.

The cut bodies of flowers travel across the world in boxes, in trucks that emit fossil fuels. The flowers end up at a wedding or on top of a casket.

What have you been taught to do? Put it away, end it, turn it into a beautiful point. But there are no more good stories. There isn't even an ending.

Outside your body, the night knits into a sweatshirt of open space around the earth. The sweatshirt enlarges every second, getting emptier and darker. Everything in the universe is wearing it, which should be useful in your new storytelling.

6 a.m.

On the last day we shared together, I got up at six in the morning. The sky was an inside-out purse, crumbs stuck to the lining. It began to let in light as I looked at the horizon beyond the apartment buildings. You descended into my pelvis.

The balance of light and dark in a day is something fundamental about nature, something hyperlocal. One day when this whole city is underwater, the day and night will follow the same pattern they've always followed.

Two months and three days after you died, we had a party. It was the solstice, the longest night of the year. All the people who had helped us came over: the midwife, the friend who told all the other friends, the ones who made the lasagna. I put on lipstick. I got drunk and felt myself temporarily abandon the scraped meat that walks around with my name.

Everything has a balance. It's either dark or it's light.

I wanted to have a party, and I also wanted everyone to acknowledge that I was the rat corpse, the drowned queen, the little goblet someone tipped over at the end.

After the party, in the crystal dark, I turned into a monument. My head rolled off from my neck and sank into the gravel. My body stood up like a statue, and the tongue in my laughing mouth was stone now. It no longer bled.

Animals

If a crow sees a human holding a dead crow

The crow's brain lights up with recognition

It wants to know what killed the other

The crow's response is practical

Even as it's outraged and perhaps grief-stricken

The crow wants to know how to protect itself

Wants to look in the face of the creature

Who caused the death of another

And announce it as fact to the crow community

In human grief the cognitive response slows

As the human brain tries to understand the event

After an interruption to its sense of pattern

We always say *I didn't think things like this happened*

The implication being *to people like us* even though death
is the only fact

But crows do not have a hard time acknowledging the fact
of death

Instead they move right into righteous anger

Becoming agitated upon seeing other crows dead

And never forgetting the circumstances

We find our own ways to tolerate what happened

I would like to be agitated

To sharpen with purpose

But instead I'm slower than I was

And have less clarity

I am angry and yet it does not sharpen me

I am angry and yet it slows me down

In the immediate aftermath we were exhausted

We slept until it was dark outside

Then we rose to cry and eat

Then we slept again until it was time to wake

Even the word *wake*

Simultaneously new and sad

I walked the length of my apartment at night

Going to pee or drink water

My absurd jelly belly deflating

As I tried to understand what happened to me

I am much stronger now than I was six eight ten
    months ago

I can look toward the future if I want to

And sometimes I do

I glance across the smoky barrier

At the winking eye of what's to come

Even though it causes me pain to move farther away

From what I consider the most emotionally significant
    event of my life

And I can't see the future anyway

I can see only my assumption of it

Optimistic yet fatal

I consider myself a positive person

Yes after everything

A crow came to see me one day in the spring

It came to my bird feeder and tapped its huge beak on the
    plastic

I had never seen such a large bird so near my home

Afterward my sister texted me *A good omen*

And I wanted it to be, I did

In 2018 an orca carried her dead calf around with her for
    seventeen days

News outlets referred to it as a "tour of grief"

After seventeen days she released the calf

And continued to swim with her pod

We had to relinquish our baby's body

So soon after her birth and death

There was not enough time to hold it

To feel its weight outside of me and to admire it

We gave her body back to the hospital staff

We had a small gathering

And then we went on a road trip

Aimlessly driving the American South

On a road trip we called our Grief Tour

Seventeen days after we had first held her

She was in a box at the funeral director's

And we were in North Carolina

That cold morning I hiked a trail to Chimney Rock

Stopping every few minutes because I was so light-headed

I was with my family

My husband, my sisters, my mother, my brother-in-law,
    my niece

I was recovering from birth and from surgery

I was coming to a lookout point

I looked down the mountain

I saw an American flag

And thought *I feel like shit*

I Think That I Would Die

Just before I went under I felt my pulse speed up. I felt a sense of panic. The anesthesiologist repeated *You feel a sense of panic,* but he didn't look at me while he was saying it. The baseline of my pulse rang out across the room, translated by a machine. A kaleidoscope of lights above my head was beautiful, it rearranged like reality every time I closed and reopened my eyes.

Just before I went under I had the most frightening thought I have ever had.

I can never tell you what it was.

There is nothing to be afraid of with anesthesia. You will be watched very closely while you are asleep. You will become the machines, the table, the air. You will feel no pain as they cut into your body.

The undertow is more powerful than anything.

Like a patient etherized upon a table: Eliot's description of the evening sky.

In the nineties, my father had a girlfriend who was an

anesthesiologist. Together they danced the foxtrot in her living room.

Just about anything can become familiar.

Insomnia

How many more hours to pretend.

The pain in my shoulders radiates into my wrists. In my brain the refrain is *I have nothing*. This is self-pitying, but in the smallest hours I let myself do it.

This poem sees me doing it.

I had been warned that after baby, I wouldn't sleep. I would be happy and desperate, delirious from the turned-up bowl of my schedule. *But it goes so fast*, everyone kept saying.

When you were inside me, some nights we used to rise together. I patted you through my skin, and knew we were a team.

When I was a child, I used to tear out fistfuls of my own hair just so I could walk out of the bedroom and tell my mother *Look what happened*. In my teenage years, I began to sleepwalk, brushing my teeth again and again. Family members would find me in the dark of the living room, staring at the clock.

In the other room, my devices pretend to sleep too. The lights from the modem blink across the ceiling as it receives packets of data. It emits a companionable hum.

Poem for Pigeon

Sometimes it's missing

A leg or an eye as it walks

Like a stubborn windup toy

Down the dirty sidewalk

Cooing eating shitting

Hiding its half-assed nest

In a raggedy bodega awning

Or building it around a row of bird-control spikes

Using the sharp metal to hold up sticks

And cigarette butts and eventually eggs

Then sitting there staring as if to say

Fuck you, I live here

Purple-gray as an exhale

From a delivery truck at dawn

Looking at the world

With the red eyes

Of the hungover

The city's own

Relatably messy little buddy

Hungry and down for whatever

No matter how undignified

Chicken bones dog food vomit

Opportunistic and ready

Just to see another day

Hurrying toward the food cart

Nearly under my feet

As I walk to my office

With my anxious stomachache

And my lunch packed in my bag

And my eggs unspooling themselves

Into nothingness day by day

I see its feathers in the flowerpot

Droppings on the windowsill

Footprints meandering like a signature across

The fresh concrete in front of the Whole Foods

As the sun rises for the millionth time

Like piss in the bladder

At a Reading Listening to a Poem About Motherhood

How are all these flowers always unfolding. Milk as an invention. A placid kind of darkness envelops you, and you exist in it as an ecosystem that sustains.

I am a hurt ecosystem. My baby is not present, so she must just be a metaphor. I'm present in the darkness too and it hurts my body. I'm trapped in the planet. The moon rolls around the sky like a peeled egg, and I shrink back as quickly as possible. There. Nobody ever even knew I wanted to touch it.

But I wanted to hold it to my eye. These two are so alike, after all. Alone in the sky like that.

I wanted to sing to it, just a little. I was sure it could hear me.

Being in a room with other mothers is to my benefit and I take it like a prescription. It's good to realize my potential, my meaning in this life. I have to grow a third tit, and it is a ghost tit to feed my baby who is a metaphor.

You say "I would like to be a real friend to you" and I can't tell if you are joking.

The darkness I am in is so full it's leaking. I have to catch it in a disposable pad I slip inside my bra. I erased the rage from this poem, but there is still rage in it. And so I failed again.

Desire to Live

When my daughter died, for a moment, I wanted to die too. The thought came to me as I began to go under anesthesia, not a thought as much as movement bubbling up from somewhere deep underneath my thoughts. When the words *I want to die* became legible from the dark substance, I could feel my heart beginning to race in my body like it, too, was afraid I meant what I was thinking. I told the anesthesiologist beside me that I was about to panic. He was working to put me under. I felt my heart beat hard inside my chest, and I closed my eyes to the pattern of lights and medical personnel shaping and reshaping itself above me. I felt the words *I want to die* hover above me like creatures in flight. I felt the air move from their wings, and then I went unconscious.

My desire to live has always been with me. I've formed my entire personality around resilience: Whatever happens to me, I can take it. Give me the worst form of punishment, the absolute shit. I'll emerge on the other side, good as new. This had worked for me for thirty-something years. I had never questioned my desire to live until the moment the medical darkness descended on the worst day of my life.

When I awakened from the procedure, my desire to live

returned with my consciousness. I knew I couldn't leave my husband alone; I knew I had to come back. The feeling swam in alongside the blood of the stranger that the doctors piped into me to replace my own lost blood. My desire to live remained firm even later, as I finally got to hold my tiny baby, the one who was now gone from me. Even then, holding her after all we'd been through, I wanted to live. Even then, looking at her face, so beautiful. Even though my path and my daughter's path diverged when I finally got to see her face, I wanted to live, and I'm grateful for this mercy, because had the desire to die come upon me at that moment, I don't know that I would have survived it.

Her death, so unexpected, is the worst thing I have ever experienced, but her birthday was also one of the best days of my life. It remains that way to me now—I recall it so fondly, up until its very last moments. All day long, from sunrise on, I labored, keeping myself focused, reminding myself that my pain was only pain, and that I was performing a function. My husband was beside me, a consummate teammate, walking with me when I was able, feeding me frozen blueberries, putting noise-canceling headphones over my ears, and giving me water and Gatorade. We spent the day together as a family, laboring to get our daughter out of me so we could all be together. We took the car ride. We got examined and checked in and praised for our efforts. Everything was exactly the way I had wanted it to be, until the second everything changed, until something was wrong and we couldn't wish our way out of it. Then there were paramedics, and there was a transfer, and there was an operating room, and there was my daughter's body brought to me as doctors and nurses and medical students I'd never met gathered around my bed, a funeral full of strangers. Then there was my husband crying as he whispered that he was proud of me.

I both wanted and did not want to keep thinking about every small detail of that day. I wanted to look at the pictures, even though I knew the outcome they contained. I wanted to say her name even though it made me cry sobs that wrenched my body so hard they felt like they were extracting something from me. I was so sad and so proud and loved my family so much. And I did not want to tell anyone that I had wanted to die for that brief and frightening moment.

But the memory of the feeling haunted me alongside the memory of her. For weeks I didn't say anything to anyone. Not the grief counselor we saw, not the family members and friends who visited us, not my husband with his fingers twined in my hair as we lay side by side in our bed. I would start to think about telling, and then my heart would begin to buzz like a wasps' nest in my rib cage. I knew the wasps were making the nest bigger every day. But I left them alone.

Days went on. Weeks. I felt it growing. *I have to tell you something*, I told my husband finally. I was in the darkness

of our bedroom. When I told him, I cried. It didn't matter
how brief the feeling was; I did not want to admit that I
had ever wanted to die. My husband held me, and I felt the
memory glide silently over me. It was the shadow of a boat
against the ocean floor.

Megalophobia

I saw a satellite roll across the sky

A steady light much higher than a plane

I say saw instead of watched because I didn't go looking
for it

Instead it entered the small window of my eyes

And I followed it as it bisected the pattern

That emerged from the blackness as my eyes adjusted

We were looking at the stars in early evening

In the Florida Keys

I lost the satellite but kept looking

The light pollution was low enough

For the scatterplot glow of the Milky Way to be visible

The horizon extended wide beyond the bridges

And the sky dragged the ocean like a dress

Stars rising from the hem of it

Like the pins in the metal cylinder

Of a music-box mechanism

The sea was the comb

That plucked each pin as it rang

Against the emptiness of the universe

The ringing was not audible

It was in my recognition

It's just something I feel

An enormity of feeling

Like the soft head of some beloved

What are you supposed to call the feeling

When you see a star and realize that it corresponds to a map

That it's just one point in a huge map

Extending over everything like an enormous dark skull

And then after a while the sky itself becomes
    overwhelming to you

Even though it's a thing you live with every day

Let everything happen to you, beauty and terror

Says Rilke, someone who died

There are the dead and there are the living

And what do the dead have to tell us

They got out of here

They don't have to do this

I am terrified all the time

I am filled with fear in the face of beautiful things

The most beautiful thing I ever saw has made me the most
    afraid

And the fear has never left me

I walk my days choosing cans at the market

I lie my nights listening to the cries of car alarms like
    melancholy dogs

And the fear still lives in me like a bead of mercury

Inscrutable mirrored and so very poisonous

And when I look up at the sky

I lose my sense of proportion

I forget where my edges are

I have the urge to sit down

And catalog what I have

Here are my two hands

And my forehead with its headlamp

The basket of my rib cage holding its small bruised fruit

And here is my husband

Tender and freckled

And warm in the dark

One hand around my waist

The other pointing up

At the constellation Draco

Maternity Coat

I walk through another winter without you

I'm wearing a coat that has another baby's spit-up on it

It's a faint outline near the collar

When it comes to clothes I am following a well-worn
    tenet:

Dress for the job you want

Sunflower

Once there was a sunflower on a fire escape across from my own. It grew slowly, as plants do, from a small pot. I did not notice it until it was huge, its big head on its small stalk, wobbling hilariously in the wind. The surprise of seeing the sunflower made me laugh. *It's so big*, I kept saying. How did I not notice.

I have a blind spot. I now know this.

In the maternity ward, there was an emblem on our door of a calla lily, the flower of funerals. The emblem was there to warn anyone entering about the atmosphere of the room. All the other rooms in the ward received sunflower emblems.

Behind my funeral door, so much of my blood was gone that I felt completely dried of everything. But urine still leaked from my catheter, a muted yellow, my body ejecting more than I thought it was capable of ejecting.

In the lily room, they gave me the blood of a stranger, and I took it and let it rehydrate my body like a plant being watered.

Sunflowers are like a total eclipse. They are dark in the middle, with a corona that extends.

During an eclipse, animals and plants go to sleep. They start to wind down, tucking their legs under their bodies, closing their leaves. Bats begin hunting. Mosquitoes start biting. When the eclipse is over, they experience stress because what happened is not what they expected.

I realize now that you came from the eclipse. You were sucked back into it when it was over, when our time together came to an end. You were beautiful and world-ending. You shocked me with your beauty, and I became so scared.

A blind spot burned into my retina. A permanent hole, like film chewed up by heat.

Sunflowers are sunny. Why wouldn't that be.

Later at the grief group, each participant brought in a flower to create a big bouquet. We were sad people in a room, and the bouquet was for all our babies. I brought in the biggest flower, a sunflower. It had the tallest stalk. It had the biggest head as it glowed there, dark in the middle.

Free

I swim in the morning, treading water in the municipal pool until my muscles fatigue. I am trying to loosen the knots that always wind their way tighter in my shoulders. This has nothing to do with you and everything to do with you. My arms open wide across the blue water, and then close again as they near my body.

It's your birthday. Today you watched from the moon as we made you a cake. Then we cried as we ate it in the living room, on our new couch with the stain-resistant fabric top.

The cake pan was the one I bought last year, before you were born. If you were here, we would have used the same pan to make your cake. Therefore the pan is like a scrying mirror into the other world. If I bake in it perfectly, I can see my life again.

There are still people who don't know that you died. I feel a mysterious pull to hold on to those people, even while I know that I can never see them again.

I have been doing nothing. I have been waiting. Pouring water after water into my body just to wait for it to exit, like a tube.

One of us said the phrase *perverse freedom*. Freedom you never wanted, freedom you feel shitty about. I am free like a flyer jammed in threes into the door of an apartment building. I am free like Buy One Get One Free. I am the one you get free.

Acknowledgments

The poem "Ursa Minor" owes a debt to this line from *Third-Millennium Heart* by Ursula Andkjær Olsen: "We have to die before we can meet. Before we can meet in all our GLORIA." I underlined this line before everything, and returned to it after.

Sarah Jean Grimm: thank you so much for everything. How lucky to get to work with a dear friend who would also care for my heart. Yuka Igarashi, and everyone on team Soft Skull: thank you for taking a chance on this book, and for helping to shape it into a beautiful object. Monika Woods: our meetings made me feel like my brain worked again. Thank you, Leia Penina Wilson at *The Fourth River*, Johannes Göransson at *Burning House Press*, Vincent James at *Denver Quarterly*, Steven Karl at *Sink Review*, and Rachael Allen at *Granta*, who published some of these poems, a few in earlier versions.

Thank you: Minna Pollari, who flew out to keep me alive in those first days. Tarja Pollari and Maija Zidek. Stewarts, Lundies, Bensons, and Seales. Joyelle McSweeney, Christine Hou, Todd Dillard, JD Scott, Eric Amling. Kyle Ashby, Amy Lasky, William Furio, Judy Berman. Amelia and Laure. Charlie Mirisola and family. The parents who attended the Pregnancy Loss Support Program in the summer of 2019, and those who ran and continue to run it. The people posting on the loneliest subreddits. The people who broke through the barrier.

Clara, my earth baby. The writing of these poems predates your time, but you are inextricably connected to them. You are someone's sister.

And finally, Michael, my partner in everything. Some days all I could do was look to you.

NIINA POLLARI is the author of
Dead Horse and the translator, from
the Finnish, of Tytti Heikkinen's *The
Warmth of the Taxidermied Animal*.
She is also an occasional reviewer. Her
work can be found at *Catapult*, *The Los
Angeles Review of Books*, *Pitchfork*, and
other outlets.